Notes on Re-Imagining Universities

Vol.01

University of Tomorrow

Reclaiming the Soul & Meaning of Academia

Prof. Bassem Khafagy

ELME Publishing
San Diego • Doha • Antalya

University of Tomorrow: *Reclaiming the Soul & Meaning of Academia*

This book is a collection of reflective works exploring the intersection of education, technology, and human wisdom as global universities confront the defining existential crisis of our time. The production of this book involved a range of modern tools and technologies, including artificial intelligence, for research assistance, content development, and editorial refinement. All final decisions regarding text, structure, tone, and intellectual direction were made exclusively by the author. The transparent use of these tools reflects the author's commitment to leveraging every available resource in service of clarity, depth, and reach. It is a deliberate practice of the technological collaboration advocated for within these very pages.

Published by
ELME Publishing - AKADIMYA GROUP

1985 Del Amo Blvd, Suite N2242, Torrance, California (CA), 90501, USA

With generous support from our academic partner: World Universities Foundation, WUF
www.wuf.global | books@wuf.global

Printed in USA
First Edition – March 2026

ISBN: 978-1-889626-26-0

Cover & Interior Design, ELME Publishing
Typography & Layout: AKADIMYA

10 9 8 7 6 5 4 3 2 1

For permissions, comments, or media inquiries, please contact:
books@wuf.global

To The Young Leaders of Tomorrow ..

The countless souls

taking their first breath

in places our academic prestigious walls

have never reached

May we have the grace

to leave behind ..

our own castles

we call "universities"

and meet you where

the future is actually beginning

CONTENTS

CONTENTS 4

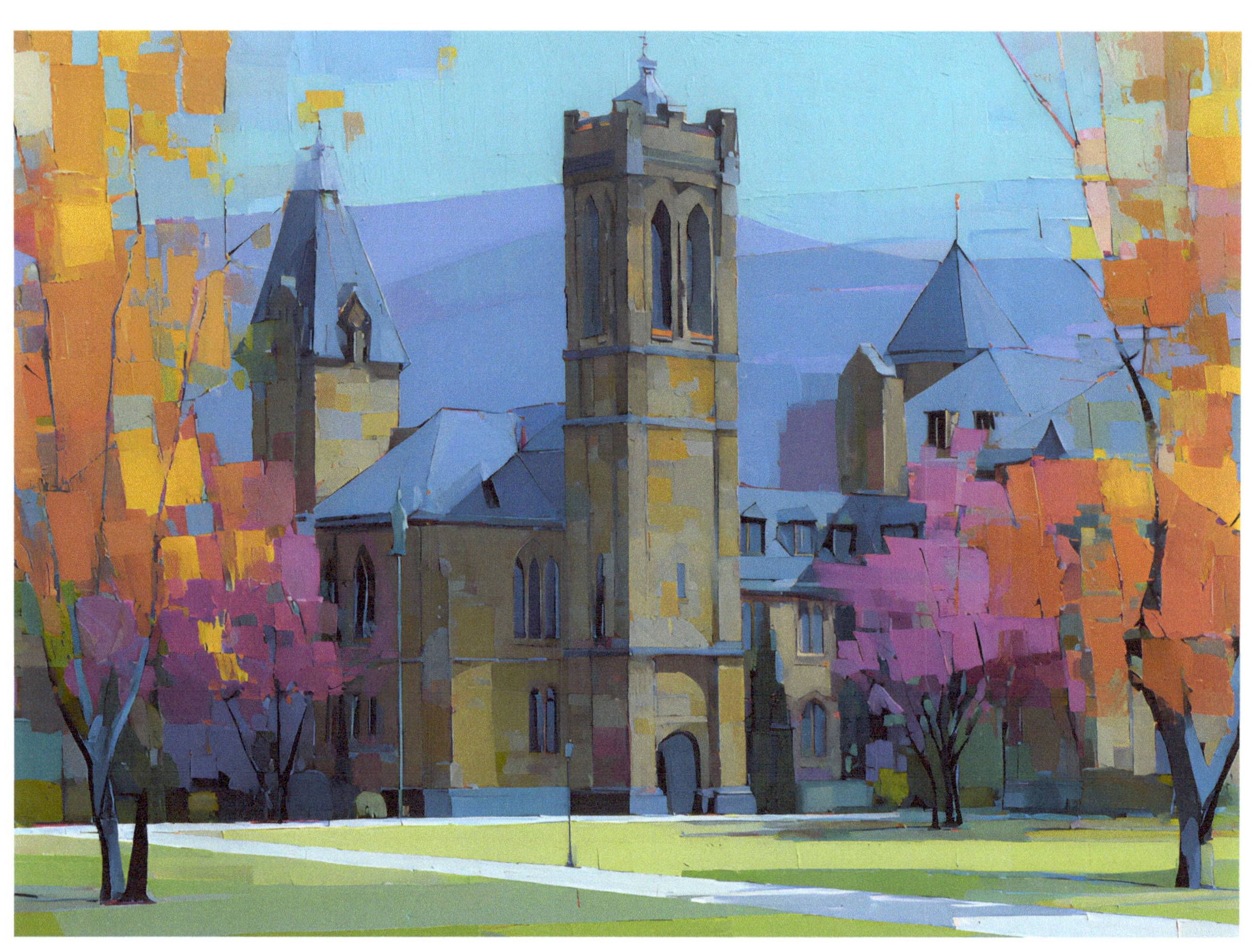

Preface

A QUIET CONVERSATION

The most profound transformations do not begin with a grand announcement, but with a quiet conversation

For forty years, I have walked through the halls of academia across different systems and countries. I have watched universities transform from sanctuaries of deep inquiry into highly competitive corporate entities. Somewhere along this journey, the noble pursuit of cultivating wisdom was quietly replaced by the frantic race for institutional status.

We became obsessed with measuring the things that matter least. We prioritized publication volume over societal impact, and we celebrated prestige while ignoring local relevance. This realization was the catalyst for my gradual transition away from traditional academic roles.

In 2025, I thought of retirement, even if partially. It did not work. Five months after this partial retirement, I decided to come back to work. At that point, I made a promise to myself and my colleagues.

I decided this new chapter in my life would not be dedicated to rest, but to channeling my energy with more focus than ever before. Many colleagues reached out with kind words and asked what would come next.

I knew the answer had been shaping itself in my mind for years. I realized that our most important academic conversation is the one we are not yet having. We spend all our time discussing a narrow fraction of the system while completely ignoring its massive foundation.

The Missing Voice

We rightly celebrate the excellence of the world's top ranked universities. These elite institutions do vital work, but they represent only one thousand out of more than thirty five thousand universities globally. I kept wondering who speaks for the vast majority of humanity that actually learns outside those prestigious walls.

Where is the collective voice for the thousands of local institutions that champion diverse cultures and transformative academicians? These unranked universities are the true lifeblood of our global society. Yet their voices are almost completely absent from the international dialogue on the future of education.

"The future of education does not lie only in a narrow elite, but in the collaborative ecosystem of our entire academic world"

My work ahead is now dedicated to helping build a powerful and unified voice for all universities. We must recognize that the future of learning relies entirely on this rich, diverse, and collaborative ecosystem. To achieve this, we cannot rely on the same closed committees that created the silence in the first place.

The world has radically changed while our institutions looked the other way. Artificial intelligence has made basic intelligence and information as abundant as water from a tap. We must evolve from being simple providers of content into deliberate designers of wisdom.

If universities do not make this shift, they risk becoming highly efficient but fundamentally irrelevant. We cannot manage the gentle decline of an old system any longer. We must become the bold architects of a completely new paradigm.

The Power of Notes

I decided this next phase of my journey would begin differently. Rather than writing a traditional academic treatise, I chose to share my thoughts through a series of short, reflective pieces. I called them notes because they were meant to be accessible, immediate, and deeply personal.

These notes were originally shared publicly to invite a global response. The goal was to explore this new direction in the open and see who else felt the exact same urgency. The response was overwhelming, proving that educators around the world are hungry for a profound shift in purpose.

"We cannot rely on closed committees to fix a silence they helped create"

This book is the culmination of those shared reflections and public dialogues. It is an attempt to gather those scattered thoughts into a single, undeniable wave of intention. We are moving beyond the fragmented noise of daily academic management to ask what we are truly here for.

The thoughts captured in these pages are not meant to be comfortable. They are designed to challenge the museum guards of academia who fight to preserve a broken status quo. They are meant to dismantle the curriculum concrete that slows human progress down to a bureaucratic crawl.

An Invitation to Act

We must stop viewing education merely as a private product and restore its status as a public promise. University is a soul in need of revival, and true revival requires immense collective courage. We need leaders, faculty, and students who are willing to act before they feel completely ready.

This collection of thoughts is an invitation to join a much larger movement. We are aspiring to build a massive global infrastructure to represent hundreds of millions of students, millions of academic staff, and all the stakeholders of higher education.

It will be a long-term initiative for at least a decade. We started the "World Universities Foundation, WUF" to become a voice for all.

We are preparing to gather annually for the "World Summit on Universities" to intentionally participate in designing the future of academia.

“The university is a soul in need of revival, and true revival requires immense collective courage”

I invite you to read these pages not as a final conclusion, but as a vital starting point. Let these notes provoke your own uncomfortable questions and inspire your own local actions. I truly believe the best is yet to come, and our real work together begins right now. Welcome aboard.

Prof. Bassem Khafagy
March 6th, 2026
Antalya, Turkiye

[01]

URGENT QUESTIONS

The most dangerous moment for any institution is when it stops asking uncomfortable questions

Something unusual is happening across global higher education today. We have more than 264 million students enrolled in over 35,000 institutions worldwide. Yet despite this massive scale and unprecedented reach, the university feels increasingly unsure of its own existential purpose.

For nearly a millennium, universities have served as the cornerstones of human progress.

They were designed to be sanctuaries for truth that fostered wisdom and shaped societies through the relentless pursuit of knowledge.

Today, we live in a time where artificial intelligence can write an essay in seconds, transforming raw knowledge into a cheap commodity.

At the same time, education is increasingly viewed as a private product rather than a public promise. This dual force of technological disruption and market logic has created a profound identity crisis within our academic halls.

We must ask if these institutions are drifting away from their foundational purpose.

The Forgotten Majority

We rightly celebrate the excellence of the world's top-ranked universities. These elite institutions command the global conversation, attract massive funding, and set the standards for academic success.

The current ranking institutions and corporations are producing annual ranking reports for only the top 1000 -1500 universities globally. Only 4.2% of all universities! We must ask who speaks for the other 34,000 institutions where the vast majority of humanity actually learns.

For too long, the narrative of higher education has been monopolized by this narrow group of one thousand institutions. Where is the collective voice for all other universities that champion diverse cultures and transformative faculty? These unranked institutions are the true lifeblood of our global society.

"The future of education does not lie only within prestigious walls, but in the collaborative ecosystem of our entire academic world"

They educate the local workforce, solve regional problems, and uplift communities that will never step foot on an elite campus. Yet they are often pressured to abandon their missions to chase the exact same metrics that define the top tier. Global rankings are driven by a billion-dollar industry that dominates institutional behavior worldwide.

This current ranking system celebrates prestige and exclusivity over the deeper impact of education on society.

It forces smaller, less funded universities to compete in a game they cannot win by measuring them against standards disconnected from their community realities. When institutions prioritize these external metrics, they lose the ability to cultivate wise and ethical leaders.

A Soul in Need of Revival

Somewhere in the relentless pursuit of performance metrics, we seem to have lost sight of our core purpose. Technology can deliver information instantly, but it cannot replicate the nuanced art of critical thinking. We are risking the loss of what made universities truly unique.

"When did the mission shift from cultivating wisdom to maintaining status?"

After decades in higher education, observing different systems and countries, I keep returning to a quiet and undeniable conclusion. The university is not simply an educational facility or a corporate entity. It is a soul in need of revival.

Revival does not mean repair or revolution. It means rediscovering something essential that has been buried under layers of bureaucracy and market logic. It means clearing up the noise and asking again what we are really here for.

A meaningful university today must do more than deliver content or confer degrees to its graduates.

It must renew its commitment to being a place where truth is pursued with courage and where progress is driven by discovery. We must reclaim the human element in higher education.

This means fostering environments where students grapple with complex problems and emerge as thoughtful citizens rather than just consumers of data. Without that moral and intellectual clarity, we risk becoming highly efficient but fundamentally irrelevant.

The Crisis of Imagination

When people talk about the crisis of universities, they usually point to funding shortages, global rankings, and digital disruption.

They worry about changing demographics and the rapid advancement of artificial intelligence. But none of these represent the real threat to our institutions.

The deeper crisis of the university is a crisis of imagination. Somewhere along the way, universities stopped asking a very simple question. Why not?

"Adaptation without imagination slowly turns into irrelevance"

Why not teach better instead of publishing more? Why not reward wisdom instead of volume, and evaluate our impact on society rather than just our position on a ranking table? These are not radical questions, but foundational ones that strike at the heart of the academic mission.

Yet many institutions no longer ask them because the system quietly discourages curiosity about purpose. It is easier to comply with rankings than to challenge what they value. It is easier to optimize performance than to rethink the entire mission of the institution.

So universities adapt efficiently and safely to the demands of the market. But adaptation without imagination slowly turns into irrelevance. The most dangerous moment for any institution is not when it is attacked or defunded, but when it stops asking uncomfortable questions about itself.

If we could build the university again from scratch today, without rankings or assumptions, we must ask what it should truly be. We must stop managing the decline of an old system and start designing the architecture of a new one.

I invite you to join this quiet conversation as we begin to re-imagine the future of our universities.

[02]

END OF SCARCITY

The Scarcity of Information is dead. The Scarcity of Wisdom is just beginning

To re-imagine this future, we must first recognize what the university has lost. For most of the past millennium, the university held a unique and powerful role in society. It was the sacred gatekeeper of knowledge, standing as the place where humanity organized, questioned, preserved, and transmitted its most valuable insights.

To walk through its halls was to access what was profoundly scarce. Books, expert scholars, and the accumulated wisdom of civilization were safely locked behind these institutional walls.

History teaches us a relentless lesson about human progress and technological evolution. The wheel of change not only creates turbulence but it also creates opportunities

What is scarce today inevitably becomes abundant tomorrow. The internet arrived, and suddenly the carefully guarded information of the world was available to anyone with a connection.

Today, a child with a smartphone holds more raw information than the great scholars of the past could gather in an entire lifetime.

Knowledge is no longer a rare treasure hidden in exclusive libraries. It has become as commonplace and instantly accessible as water from a tap.

If the value of the university was built on organizing and dispensing this knowledge, we must ask what happens when anyone can access it instantly.

We are entering an era where the university can no longer define itself solely by what it knows.

The Breached Moat

We must face the uncomfortable truth that our defensive academic moat has been breached twice over.

First, knowledge became a commodity, and universities adapted by claiming they taught students how to process that information. We proudly stated that we did not just teach facts, but rather we taught students how to think.

Now, intelligence itself is becoming a commodity following the exact same path as

information. Artificial intelligence can analyze, synthesize, reason, and solve complex problems faster than most human minds.

The very cognitive skills that universities spent decades developing in students can now be replicated by algorithms. Additionally, artificial intelligence is advancing at an astonishing pace, doubling its capabilities every seven months.

"The university of tomorrow cannot survive as a content provider. It must become a context provider"

That cornerstone of academic scarcity is now available on demand, at scale, and for a fraction of the cost. The skills we once measured to

grant degrees are being absorbed by machines.

We see this clearly in the act of writing, which was once considered the rarest of talents.

To capture knowledge or feeling in language was an extraordinary gift, but today digital tools make writing accessible to nearly everyone. Sentences and entire essays can be generated instantly.

The old definition of literacy is fading because the ability to form words is no longer a rare product, but a raw tool. The value will no longer lie in who can produce words or process basic data. It will lie in who can shape ideas, reflections, and meaning that actually deserve those words.

Currently, 78% of organizations report using artificial intelligence, and 90% of workers say it saves them time.

A person may not need to be a writer in the traditional sense, but they will desperately need to be a thinker and a synthesizer. The true graduate of tomorrow will be a curator of meaning, standing at the end of thought where reflections are framed and wisdom becomes guidance.

It is already happening. Up to 88% of students are already using generative tools for their studies and assessments. However, despite this rapid adoption, fewer than 10% of schools and universities have formal institutional policies on artificial intelligence use.

The Coffee Commodity

If knowledge and basic intelligence are no longer scarce products, the university must radically rediscover its fundamental value. We can understand this necessary transformation by looking at the global history of coffee.

For decades, coffee was a simple commodity valued only for its caffeine, sold cheaply, and traded across the world.

Then a massive cultural and economic shift occurred. Modern brands did not invent the coffee bean or change the raw material, but they wrapped it in a compelling experience.

They turned a simple beverage into a daily ritual, a designated space, and a profound sense of belonging. Coffee became much more than a drink when it became synonymous with meaning and connection. This is exactly the path that higher education must now take to survive the artificial intelligence revolution. Lectures, textbooks, and basic assessments are our coffee beans.

They are absolutely essential to the academic process, yet they are entirely abundant and replaceable. The university cannot survive by simply offering these beans to a new generation of students. We must evolve from a provider of knowledge into a deliberate designer of wisdom.

Designers of Wisdom

When anyone can access information instantly, the function of knowing is permanently outsourced to machines. What remains for

higher education is something far more subtle, human, and enduringly valuable. We are left with the urgent task of cultivating wisdom and ethical judgment.

Artificial intelligence might easily calculate how to build a bridge, but it cannot tell you if that bridge is the right solution for a community's soul. Wisdom is the application of intelligence through the lens of human values and long-term ethics. It is not merely information with time added to it.

It is the deep discernment required to navigate complexity, connect disparate disciplines, and ask the right questions in the first place. Wisdom does not scale the way data does, because it must be taught, modeled, and experienced from person to person.

"Our role is no longer to provide what is scarce, but to shape what is abundant into what is valuable"

This reality demands that we move toward what we must call the Experience and Wisdom University. In this new era, the classroom is no longer a place where scarce facts are transmitted to passive listeners. It must become a vibrant stage where abundant knowledge is shaped into identity, meaning, and true insight.

The ultimate product of higher education is not the printed diploma we hand out at graduation. The true product is the immersive journey of growth, ethical reflection, and human connection that no algorithm could ever replicate.

Institutions that cling to the old model of only offering knowledge as a product will slowly fade into irrelevance. But those that craft experiences to turn information into wisdom will lead the next chapter in humanity's intellectual journey.

[03]

THE GHOST IN THE LECTURE HALL

The future of higher education is not a destination. It is a distribution!

The next chapter, or the university of tomorrow, will not only be defined by what we teach, but by who will be sitting in our classrooms.

Imagine the year is 2045. A professor in a prestigious European university walks into a lecture hall designed for three hundred students.

Only twelve young people are sitting there, and the silence in the room is not just quiet. It is entirely demographic. For decades, academia has operated under a hopeful but flawed philosophy.

We believed that if we simply built the campus, the world would inevitably come. Universities measure their success in five-year strategic plans and celebrate their prestige through annual global rankings. But long before any of those metrics matter, there is a quieter force already shaping the future of higher education.

We built what we can call the Al-Qalaa, or the fortress. These were isolated and prestigious spaces crowded with the exact same traditional demographic we have served for centuries.

But while we were busy polishing our ivory towers, the world was quietly moving its center of gravity. A close look at global births for a single year reveals a roadmap for the survival or extinction of the modern university.

The Shifting Center

The data reveals a world that has radically changed shape while our institutions looked the other way. Africa is rapidly becoming the world's largest supplier of future students, workers, and citizens.

Nations like Nigeria are now producing more human potential in a single year than the entirety of the European continent.

"Nigeria (7.6 million births) is now producing more human potential than the entirety of Europe (6.2 million births)"

India is adding a new student body every year that dwarfs the growth of other major global powers. Meanwhile, the Western world accounts for barely a fraction of the globe's new arrivals.

Europe appears small today not because it has suddenly declined, but because it has entered a different demographic phase shaped entirely by aging societies and low fertility rates.

"Demography creates immense pressure long before it creates opportunity"

Births are the very beginning of the academic journey. Before we debate research output or artificial intelligence, there are classrooms that must exist and teachers who must be trained. These institutions must scale in regions where resources are limited and educational demand is absolutely immense.

A country with millions of births does not automatically gain global strength or economic prosperity. It gains an incredible responsibility that depends entirely on access to quality higher education. Whether that massive youth population turns into a demographic dividend or a long-term crisis relies on what universities decide to do right now.

The Extraction Economy

For a long time, the global higher education model has functioned as a massive extraction economy. We wait for the brightest minds to save their money, navigate complex visas, and fly to smaller demographic bubbles, in a small number of cities and countries.

The west has effectively harvested top talent from the developing world to sustain the academic prestige of the developed world.

This traditional model is becoming morally and practically unsustainable. The math of relying on international student mobility simply no longer works when the vast majority of human potential is concentrated far away from legacy campuses.

Furthermore, extracting the brightest minds often leaves their home countries without the talent desperately needed to solve local problems.

"If ninety percent of your future students are born where you have no footprint, your prestige is actually a perimeter"

We must ask ourselves if universities are preparing for the students who will actually arrive in fifteen years. Or are we still optimizing for prestige within shrinking, aging systems? Rankings reward historical advantage, but demography exposes future obligation.

The most important transformation ahead is not technological, but purely demographic. This challenge cannot be solved by competition between elite universities fighting over a shrinking pool of traditional applicants.

It requires new models of deep cooperation between institutions in high-capacity regions and those facing explosive global demand. The global university community must pause and reflect on where its true duty lies.

Beyond the Fortress

Universities that will thrive in the future must realize that the fortress mindset is permanently over. We cannot stay tucked away in our increasingly empty castles of knowledge waiting for the world to find us.

We must move toward decentralized learning hubs that prioritize accessible wisdom over a physical seat in a legacy lecture hall.

Digital connection is no longer just a feature we offer as a convenient alternative to the classroom. It is the fundamental environment of modern learning. We must meet these millions of future students exactly where they live, rather than expecting them to cross oceans and overcome financial barriers to reach us.

"The future of the university will be decided by who shows up where humanity is growing"

The job of top universities is no longer to act as gatekeepers filtering the world to find a few lucky students. They must become enablers who fuel the world by exporting knowledge infrastructure to where the human life actually is. The center of gravity for humanity has permanently shifted, and academia must have the courage to shift with it.

If universities do not adapt to this reality, we are not just losing enrollment numbers or tuition revenue.

Academia will be losing relevance to the story of the twenty-first century. We are failing the fundamental promise of education to uplift society.

The ghost in the lecture hall is a warning we must heed today. We must stop building walls around our knowledge and start building bridges to the youth who will inherit this earth.

The university must leave the fortress and finally rejoin the world.

[04]

THE CURRICULUM CONCRETE

The degree is supposed to be a launchpad, not a time capsule

For universities to rejoin the world, we must first dismantle the barriers that keep us trapped inside our own structures. There is a quiet illusion many of us live with in higher education today. We read books, attend seminars, and accumulate continuous certifications.

Yet years pass without a single meaningful project being tested in the real world. Our thinking becomes sharper, and our academic frameworks multiply.

The deeper issue is that learning has quietly transformed from a starting point into a completely safe destination.

We postpone real action behind highly respectable excuses. We convince ourselves that taking just one more workshop or reading one more book is necessary preparation.

We tell ourselves that this delay is actually wisdom. What accumulates is simply knowledge, completely disconnected from any real momentum.

The problem is rarely a lack of information. We live in the most information-rich moment in all of human history. What we are truly facing is a profound fear of friction and ambiguity. We must confront how our educational structures enable this exact fear.

The Speed Crisis

The real threat to higher education is a bureaucratic structure we can call Curriculum Concrete. This is the rigid system of academic committees and credit hours that makes it nearly impossible for universities to adapt.

The traditional degree is hardening into something inflexible, and its true value is rapidly dissolving.

We must consider the catastrophic speed differential between global industry and our academic institutions.

A transformative technology like generative artificial intelligence evolves with breathtaking speed. New models and profound capabilities are launching into the world every few weeks.

The skills required for success change just as quickly. Essential competencies like prompt engineering, ethical artificial intelligence use, and digital verification are becoming mandatory for survival.

"By the time a new course clears every committee hurdle, the technology it addresses is already obsolete"

Meanwhile, it takes the average large university several years just to formally approve a single new interdisciplinary course. This slow crawl is not born from deliberate malice.

It is the natural inertia of a massive bureaucracy designed for stability rather than agility. This vacuum of guidance ensures that institutional inertia remains the default operating model.

The result is a fundamentally devalued educational product. We are graduating students into a world that is rapidly transforming.

Yet only a fraction of those students were formally taught how to use new technologies critically within their chosen discipline.

The gap between what the world demands and what the curriculum provides grows wider every single day.

The Illusion of Readiness

Much of what we now call academic preparation is actually a form of protection. Learning becomes a comfortable shelter from uncertainty. It protects us from public judgment and from the terrifying possibility of being wrong. Entire academic industries are built around sustaining this perpetual state of preparation.

For decades, formal education systems have reinforced a strictly linear belief about human growth. We taught students that they must fully prepare before they are allowed to act.

We taught them that mistakes are absolute failures rather than valuable data points. We rewarded correct answers far more than we rewarded brave attempts.

"Readiness is not a prerequisite for action. It is often the result of it"

We elevated experts who simply know things over practitioners who actually build things. The outcome of this system is visible everywhere we look. We see graduates who wait for permission instead of experimenting with their ideas. We see professionals who feel unready despite accumulating years of impressive credentials.

We have created an entire generation of brilliant minds permanently stuck in rehearsal mode. Becoming a professional learner offers tremendous comfort. It provides social approval, clear milestones, and incredibly low risk. Action offers none of those comforts.

Real action brings only ambiguity, exposure, loneliness, and inevitable criticism. Yet action is where true human growth actually happens.

Agile Education

Higher education institutions must urgently shift their focus away from protecting the rigid structure of the degree. We must redirect all our energy toward maximizing the value of the graduate.

This requires replacing curriculum concrete with agile education. We must prioritize demonstrable skills and project-based work over mere seat-time requirements.

"The future does not need more perfect students. It needs bold practitioners"

Academic departments need immediate and iterative control over their course content. This will allow them to reflect current trends and adapt to technological shifts instantly.

We must force curriculum review to be fast, cross-disciplinary, and tied closely to external industry advisory boards. Universities must stop operating in isolated academic silos.

As we speak about the future of higher education, we must ask a critical question. Are we preparing people merely to understand the world, or to actually engage with it?

If institutions continue to optimize for completion and correctness alone, they will produce exceptional learners who hesitate at the edge of reality. We must transition from preparing people until they are ready, to actively supporting them while they are not.

We must dissolve the concrete before the next generation finds their qualifications completely obsolete the moment they step into the workplace. The university was meant to be a launchpad. We must ensure it does not become a monument to the past.

I ask this of myself as much as I ask it of the entire academic system. We must stop hiding behind learning and finally begin to engage with the world.

[05]

RETHINKING THE ELITE

Maybe the real elite is the one that serves, uplifts, and matters

This true engagement requires us to fundamentally rethink the metrics we use to define academic success. We freely give the title of elite to certain universities today. We do this usually because they are exceptionally large, incredibly wealthy, and produce an impressive volume of academic research.

We see them sitting comfortably at the very top of international rankings and treat them as the ultimate standard of success.

But we must remember that research is merely a tool rather than an ultimate purpose. Science is a powerful instrument for understanding the world, but it is not the sole goal of human existence.

Carrying or producing an elegant tool does not automatically make a person or an institution truly elite.

We have confused the possession of vast resources with the possession of a noble soul. The global higher education system has become obsessed with a very narrow and sterile definition of prestige.

We measure financial endowments, physical infrastructure, and publication counts to determine which institutions deserve our admiration.

Yet these cold metrics tell us absolutely nothing about the moral character or the societal value of the university itself.

We must fundamentally rethink what we praise and what we choose to value. A university is meant to be a guiding light for society, not merely a factory for citations.

The Illusion of Prestige

We must ask difficult and uncomfortable questions about the moral compass of these prestigious institutions. If a university actively supports violence or remains entirely silent about the mass killing of children, we must fundamentally question its elite status. Prestige without deeply held human principles is simply organized hypocrisy.

If women are systematically excluded from real leadership roles, that elite status is a total illusion. If faculty members are repeatedly denied promotion because of their faith, race, or skin color, the institution fails its most basic human test. An institution cannot claim to represent the pinnacle of human thought while practicing the lowest forms of discrimination.

Furthermore, a university cannot be elite if it completely ignores the profound daily struggles of its own city and surrounding region. Chasing global prestige instead of local purpose is a tragic betrayal of the foundational academic mission. We must ask who actually decides what the word elite means in our modern world.

"Carrying an elegant tool does not make an institution elite"

Are these definitions created by elite people, by the universities themselves, or by the communities they are supposedly designed to serve? The current system answers this question by looking entirely inward. It protects its own status rather than lifting the communities that desperately need its wisdom.

A Different Standard

Years ago, during an academic trip to Malaysia, I visited a small university located far from any major city. It had absolutely no global ranking, no massive research output, and no recognizable international brand. Yet in the eyes of its surrounding community, it was the ultimate beacon of hope and progress.

It educated their young talent and addressed their real, daily problems. It created tangible solutions for its specific region and lifted the lives of everyone around it. It proved that it truly mattered to the people who needed its presence the most.

So we must honestly ask ourselves which institution is the true elite university. Maybe the real elite is not the biggest, the richest, or the loudest institution competing in the global market. Maybe the real elite is the one that serves its people and fundamentally matters to the human beings standing right outside its doors.

True elitism should be measured by the depth of a university's service, not the height of its administrative tower. When an institution roots itself deeply in its community, it achieves a lasting relevance that no international ranking could ever bestow. The ultimate measure of an institution is how much darkness it removes from the world.

The Missing Judges

Also, let us look at the elite status from a different perspective; measuring quality. When we speak about quality in higher education today, we almost always look upward for validation.

We look to international rankings, prestigious accreditation bodies, and national quality agencies to tell us if we are succeeding. These agencies almost always measure the exact same two things, which are teaching mechanisms and research output.

"True elitism is measured by the depth of service,
not the height of a tower."

But there is something deeply strange and fundamentally flawed about this arrangement. In nearly every other industry in the world, quality is ultimately judged by the customer and the primary user. Only in universities do we systematically exclude the main user of the institution, who is the student.

We do not seriously ask students to tell us whether the university is fair, or whether its governance is transparent.

We rarely ask if the campus is truly humane, if the institution actually listens to them, or if it prepares them for life rather than just for exams. We ignore the reality of the daily educational experience.

"That is not quality assurance. That is quality avoidance"

When students do manage to speak up about their experiences, we often treat their voices as emotional, immature, or entirely irrelevant.

We dismiss their lived reality in favor of abstract spreadsheets and carefully manicured institutional metrics.

By silencing the student voice, we have built a massive quality assurance industry that measures almost everything except the actual human impact of the university.

We have created a system that protects the institution from the very people it was built to serve. The university exists entirely to shape the student, yet the student is given absolutely no power to shape the university.

There are very few universities in the world today that truly measure their quality primarily through the structured and respected judgment of their students.

We rely heavily on external validation instead of internal truth, choosing comfortable metrics instead of deep institutional meaning. If we are serious about total quality in universities, students must finally move from the margins to the center of the academic conversation. They must be treated not merely as passive feedback providers or numbers on a satisfaction survey.

They must be recognized as legitimate, authoritative judges of institutional quality. In the end, it is not the international rankings that reveal true quality or institutional soul.

It is not the external agencies that experience the daily, breathing life of the university campus.

It is the students who live the reality of our institutions every single day. They alone can tell us if we are succeeding in our mission to build wise and capable citizens. We must stop looking upward to agencies and start looking inward to our own classrooms to find the truth.

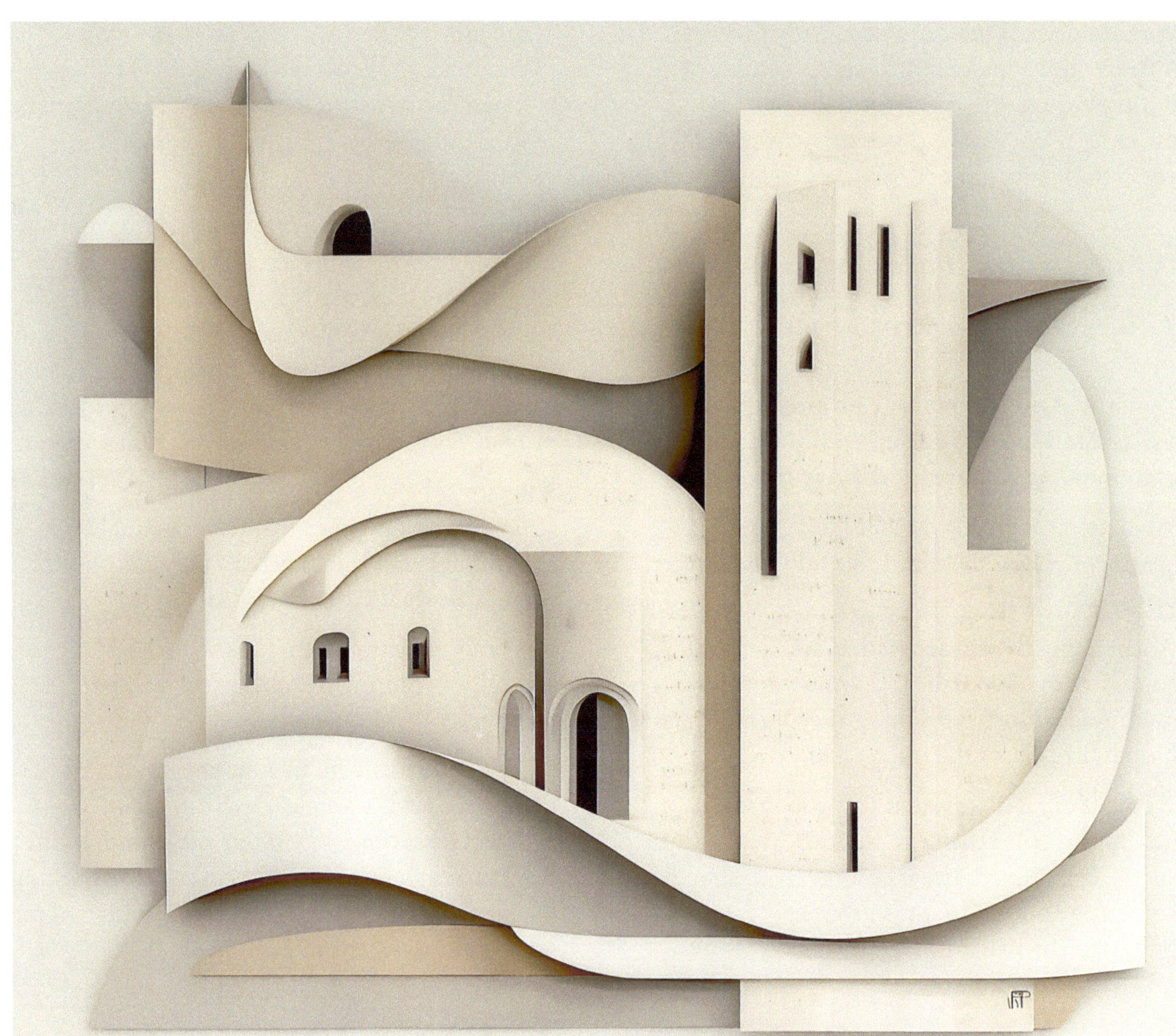

[06]

DECOLONIZING KNOWLEDGE

History did not go dark; it merely moved its brightest lamps to places our textbooks often forget to mention

Seeking and finding this truth and building on it requires us to look honestly at how we treat the foundations of human thought. We have criminalized the very mechanism that built human civilization.

In modern academia, the concept of "copying" for example has become a scarlet letter equated with laziness and intellectual bankruptcy.

We have built entire industries around detecting and punishing it, causing students to live in constant fear.

Yet we are missing a fundamental truth about human progress and discovery. The reality is that building upon previous work is exactly how knowledge actually advances. Isaac Newton did not wake up one morning and reinvent calculus from scratch.

He copied what previous generations of mathematicians had established and then pushed those concepts further.

Every scientific breakthrough begins precisely where someone else ended. Every major global innovation stands firmly on borrowed intellectual foundations.

Open-source software drives our a significant percentage of the entire digital world today, and it thrives entirely on this exact principle.

Developers copy existing code libraries, modify them, improve them, and share them back with the global community.

This is not theft but rather the beautiful mechanics of collective human intelligence.

The Cumulative Commons

The university itself is a massive monument to this structured sharing of existing knowledge. Literature reviews systematically compile what others have already discovered so we can understand the current academic landscape. We call this building on existing research when we do it properly with careful citations.

The mechanism of gathering and reusing previous thought is completely identical to what we often punish. The real question is not whether we copy, because we all do so constantly and necessarily.

The question is whether we acknowledge our sources, transform the ideas, and contribute back to the global commons.

"We are where we are today not despite copying, but because of it"

When we teach students to fear building upon existing work, we teach them to fear the cumulative nature of knowledge itself. We should instead be teaching the vital ethics of attribution and transformation.

We must abandon the pure fantasy of complete originality and embrace how understanding truly evolves. Other cultures in the world understand the value and nature of knowledge as a free source, not as only a commercial products.

This brings us to a profound misunderstanding of history that academia continues to perpetuate today.

To understand the future of global knowledge, we must first decolonize our conception of time and historical progress. We must dismantle the narratives that elevate one region while erasing the brilliance of others.

The Myth of the Dark Ages

There is a false believe in some western intellectual circles that academia, and all its tools, processes, and rules, started as a "western" phenomenon. But this is not true.

They often speak of the Dark Ages as if the sun dimmed across the entire planet between the fall of Rome and the dawn of the Renaissance. We picture a thousand years of ignorance, cultural stagnation, and complete intellectual silence. But we must ask a very simple and unsettling question about this historical framing.

For whom was the world truly dark during these centuries? This term is not an objective historical reality, but rather a convenient construct created by a specific region.

It was a mirror Europe held up to define itself by what it was not, portraying itself as the beacon while the rest of the world was in shadow.

While parts of Western Europe grappled with political fragmentation, the rest of the world

was experiencing an absolute explosion of innovation. The Islamic Golden Age saw scholars preserving and expanding upon the very sciences that Europe had tragically lost.

While the largest libraries in Northern Europe held only a few hundred books, the great library of Islamic Córdoba boasted hundreds of thousands of volumes.

During India's Gupta period, brilliant mathematicians like Aryabhatta defined the concept of zero.

This profound realization created the mathematical void that makes all modern calculation and digital technology possible today.

In the Americas, the Maya civilization was perfecting complex hieroglyphic writing and astronomical calendars of terrifying precision.

Referring to the past of all "other" nations as dark or barbaric, colonial powers actively tried to justify their global dominance.

This rhetoric of darkness was so potent that it was eventually adopted globally, erasing the pluralistic foundations of human civilization.

It reduced vibrant cultures to mere objects of conquest, stripped of their agency and their massive intellectual contributions.

When we uncritically use this terminology in academia, we perpetuate a geography of knowledge that centers one region's struggles as the universal human experience.

"By labeling the past of others as dark, colonial powers tried to justify their dominance"

We must recognize that knowledge did not disappear, but simply moved to other civilizations. History did not go dark, it merely shifted its focus to places that our modern textbooks ignore.

Intellectual Mono-culture

This historical erasure connects directly to a modern crisis we are currently witnessing in the global university system. We have created a strict intellectual mono-culture that actively filters out global genius.

For example, an overwhelming majority of all scientific research today is published exclusively in the English language.

Yet only a small fraction of the global population actually speaks English, and far fewer speak it at an academic level. The university sector effectively tells most of the world that their ideas do not count unless they can translate them perfectly.

Language is not merely a neutral tool for communication, but a profound framework for human cognition.

The structure of a language deeply affects how its speaker views and solves problems in the real world. When brilliant minds are forced to flatten their culturally nuanced thoughts into English, we lose the vital metadata of their wisdom. We strip away the unique problem-solving angles that their native languages naturally provide.

"A true global university should be a translator of worlds, not an enforcer of uniformity"

By maintaining English as the sole gatekeeper of academic validity and ranking, we are creating a completely false meritocracy. We are prioritizing linguistic privilege over raw intellectual potential and human insight.

We must wonder how many brilliant solutions to climate change, poverty, or disease are currently locked inside rejected research papers due to limited English-language proficiency.

These papers are often dismissed by major academic journals not for bad science, but simply for bad grammar. If we truly want to solve humanity's hardest problems, we need humanity's full cognitive diversity.

We must invest in artificial intelligence tools for real-time translation in academic journals and global conferences.

Scholars must be allowed to publish in their native tongues while remaining globally accessible to the wider academic community.

A true global university should be a translator of worlds rather than an enforcer of strict uniformity. We must stop filtering out genius and finally embrace the full, diverse chorus of human wisdom.

[07]

MENTORS, NOT MONITORS

A professor is a mentor and a guide, not a criminal investigator

Artificial Intelligence is changing the relationship between students and professors in more than one way. Embracing this change means fundamentally changing how we view our students and the modern tools they bring into our classrooms. In every technological revolution, there are those who choose to guard the old gates.

In academia today, we are witnessing a strange and counterproductive performance unfolding across our campuses. Professors are being pushed into an impossible and frankly degrading role as detectives and cheat police.

A professor is a teacher, a mentor, and a guide whose primary mission is to open minds. Their purpose is not to search digital bags for stolen sentences or interrogate the origin of every typed word.

Yet the sudden emergence of artificial intelligence has profoundly confused the entire academic world.

Instead of asking how we can elevate human learning, we are obsessively asking how we can catch those who cheated. When artificial intelligence detectors flag historical documents like the Declaration of Independence as machine generated, the message is absolutely clear. We are fighting the wrong battle entirely.

Professors today spend their days hunting for violations and mislabeled assignments. These detection tools are already proving to be highly unreliable and deeply flawed. They mislabel original work, they over flag certain students, and in the process, they create fear and unnecessary tension.

The Museum Guards

We have created a culture of Museum Guards within our educational institutions. These are professors and administrators so dedicated to preserving the past that they see generative technology merely as a threat to be banned.

When an institution reacts to new tools by reverting to handwritten papers and oral defenses, they are ignoring a critical reality.

The modern workplace has already moved on and fully integrated these powerful tools. Our students are stepping into a professional landscape that demands high technological fluency and rapid adaptation. The gap between student reality and institutional readiness is stark and growing wider every single day.

I have noticed an interesting paradox where professors are genuinely upset that students now write better essays with machine assistance. We must interrogate this reaction more carefully and ask what we are truly measuring.

"The controversy isn't about cheating. It's about control"

Perhaps what makes educators uncomfortable is not that technology writes well, but that it exposes our outdated metrics. It reveals how much of traditional assessment was never really about deep thinking at all. It was largely about performance, following formats, and demonstrating compliance with academic conventions.

Transformation always threatens those heavily invested in the status quo, making this a battle over control rather than true academic integrity.

The Guilt Syndrome

This relationship with technology brings another important aspect. The fear of openly using the new technologies in academia has birthed what we can call the Guilt Syndrome among brilliant minds.

I see talented authors and researchers furtively using the most powerful creative tools of our generation, only to meticulously hide their tracks. We are treating our partnership with intelligent systems as if it were an act of academic infidelity.

We benefit from this collaboration in private, but we refuse to acknowledge our partner in public. This intellectual dishonesty is not only ridiculous, it is a direct hindrance to human progress. Hiding our creative process does not protect our integrity, it actually erodes the trust we share.

"To be ashamed of your tools is to be ashamed of your own time"

Using a new tool is not a betrayal of your craft, but the very essence of human evolution. Did the Renaissance painter who used advanced optical tools to perfect their perspective commit artistic infidelity? Did the great novelist who embraced the typewriter over the quill pen cheat on literature?

The source of this guilt is a flawed and highly romanticized notion of authorship. True authorship does not lie in the manual labor of typing every single word or chipping every stone. It lies entirely in the vision, the curation, the taste, and the intellectual direction of the final work.

You are the director of your thoughts, and artificial intelligence is simply your most skilled cinematographer.

My true value lives in my thinking, my insights, and my synthesis of incredibly complex global problems.

If technology enables me to express those ideas better and faster, that is not a shortcut, it is powerful leverage.

Curators of Meaning

There was a time when writing itself was the rarest of talents and an extraordinary gift. To be able to take thoughts and set them down in words was a kind of power.

But scarcity does not last forever, and today digital tools make writing accessible to nearly everyone.

The old definition of literacy is fading because the ability to form words is no longer a rare product, but a raw tool. This does not diminish the role of writers or thinkers; it radically transforms it.

The value will no longer lie in who can produce words, but in who can shape ideas that actually deserve those words.

"The future belongs to educators who curate critical thinking rather than guard an obsolete status quo"

What will matter is not the mechanical ability to form sentences, but the courage to form insight and vision. A person may not need to be a writer in the traditional sense, but they will desperately need to be a synthesizer. The true graduate of tomorrow is less a producer of words and more a curator of meaning.

For those of us working at the intersection of education and innovation, this moment demands radical honesty. We must separate the authentic intellectual work of ethical judgment from the mechanical work that machines now handle brilliantly.

The students using these tools transparently are not the problem. They are actually the pioneers of a new global literacy.

The goal of higher education is not to train students to avoid technology entirely. It is to teach them how to use the most powerful tools available ethically, critically, and effectively. Our focus must urgently shift from detection and policing to preparation and active guidance.

We must teach students how to evaluate generated content for bias, accuracy, and depth. We must turn them into sophisticated users who can structure complex queries to achieve meaningful output.

Universities must shift from policing artificial intelligence to actively teaching its ethics and integration.

Students do not need constant surveillance; they need profound guidance to live ethically in an automated world. They need to understand how to add their own judgment, emotion, and creativity to the final product. Let us return professors to their rightful role in the academic ecosystem as mentors and guides.

They should spend their days building capable people, not building disciplinary cases. The future of education will not be saved by sophisticated detectors, but by sophisticated human conversations. We must step away from the gates of the past and become the necessary guides to the future.

[08]

THE ACADEMIC EVOLUTION

The PhD of the future is not a thesis. It is a capacity

To truly guide students into the future, we must change what we ask them to create. A century ago, the traditional doctoral dissertation was an absolute necessity for human progress. It functioned essentially as humanity's primary memory drive. In a world where information was scarce and

communication was slow, we needed scholars to meticulously capture and preserve knowledge in physical volumes.

To earn the highest academic degree meant spending years in isolated archives gathering data that few others could access. The resulting three-hundred-page document was a triumph of endurance and a vital contribution to the global library. But today, knowledge no longer needs preserving in that same static way.

Information now updates itself constantly and multiplies exponentially across digital networks. The complex answers we once spent years compiling are now instantly accessible through simple technological prompts.

This profound reality forces us to ask a difficult question about our highest academic achievements.

Are traditional dissertations still doing the job they were created for? If the original purpose of the dissertation was to retain knowledge, that specific mission is now completely over. We must acknowledge that the mechanics of capturing information have been permanently outsourced to machines.

The Measure of Depth

For centuries, universities have measured academic excellence almost entirely in pages. We have trained generations of scholars to equate intellectual depth with physical length. We operated under the rigid assumption that true wisdom could only live within dense academic text.

We built massive institutional structures that reward the volume of publication over the tangible impact of the work. Brilliant minds are forced to spend years writing about problems rather than actively solving them. But the world today desperately needs a completely different kind of depth.

"We must stop equating intellectual depth with physical length, or page count"

The traditional doctoral journey is often a highly solitary pursuit. Scholars isolate themselves for years to produce a document that is ultimately read by only a handful of committee members.

This system traps our highest intellectual potential inside a closed loop of academic validation. We are losing countless brilliant innovations to the dusty shelves of university archives.

Humanity needs the depth of usefulness and the depth of real creation. We need bold ideas that can actually be transformed into tools, medicines, technologies, and tangible social solutions.

If the ultimate goal of higher education is to advance human thinking, then the future of the doctoral degree must radically evolve.

We are already beginning to see this necessary shift happen globally. Pioneering educational systems are now allowing doctoral candidates to graduate by presenting a working product instead of a traditional long thesis. This is not a lowering of academic standards.

It is a profound recognition of what the modern world actually requires to survive and thrive. A working product can carry just as much intellectual weight as a written thesis. In many cases, it carries significantly more because it must survive the friction of reality.

The Working Product

Creating a solution that functions in the real world demands rigorous research, constant testing, and profound conceptual understanding. It requires the scholar to step out of the theoretical realm and engage directly with the messy complexities of human life. This evolution does not diminish the prestige of academia.

When a scholar builds a working product, they are forced to collaborate across different disciplines. They must consider design, ethics, human behavior, and practical implementation. This multidisciplinary approach is exactly how real innovation occurs in the modern global economy.

> *"The purpose of the university is to advance humanity, not to protect academic traditions"*

It actively breaks down the rigid silos that have artificially separated academic departments for centuries.

Embracing the working product actually expands the entire horizon of higher education. It serves as a vital reminder that the ultimate purpose of the university is not to blindly protect old traditions. The purpose is to actively advance humanity through meaningful contribution.

We must realize that the true value of doctoral study is no longer in producing a massive document. The true value lies entirely in producing a specific kind of mind. We need to cultivate minds capable of profound insight, striking originality, and applied wisdom.

These are the exact human traits that no database and no artificial intelligence can ever replace. A machine can write three hundred pages of synthesized research in a matter of seconds. But a machine cannot step into a struggling community and build a working solution that heals a specific human pain.

A Way of Seeing

The modern academic degree must transition from being a static thesis to becoming a dynamic human capacity. It should represent a unique way of seeing the world and a highly practical method of contributing to it.

We must think of better modern ways to grant these degrees that align with real human progress.

A degree should be a lasting testament to a person's ability to navigate ambiguity and create value. When we free our doctoral students from the mandate of only producing a physical book, we unlock their true creative potential. We give them permission to be inventors, social architects, and visionary leaders. This is how we return the university to its rightful place as the engine of societal transformation.

"The real value is in producing a mind capable of insight, not a document"

Artificial intelligence is not going to solve our greatest global challenges alone. It simply cannot do that because it lacks ethical judgment and lived experience. Only highly developed human minds, equipped with both advanced technology and deep empathy, can navigate the complexities of our future.

The scholar of tomorrow will not be judged by the thickness of their bound thesis on a library shelf. They will be judged by the functionality of their ideas and the positive disruption they bring to society. True academic rigor is found in the courage to build something that actually matters.

Universities that understand this fundamental shift will lead the next century of global innovation. Those that refuse to adapt will continue training brilliant scholars for a world that simply no longer exists. We must choose whether we want to build archives of the past or actively design the future.

[09]

THE CRAB BUCKET CLIMATE

They say: if I cannot achieve massive success, I will ensure that neither can you!

Designing a better future for universities is impossible if our internal environments actively punish the people trying to build it. The true obstacle to innovation in our universities is rarely a lack of

funding or a shortage of talent. It is a deeply ingrained culture of enforced mediocrity that quietly suffocates ambition across our campuses.

We can call this toxic and pervasive environment the Crab Bucket Climate. The unwritten rule of this environment is brutally simple and highly destructive. This culture goes far beyond simple professional jealousy among some academic peers.

It functions as a profound institutional mechanism dedicated to belittling the prominent and ensuring no one steps out of line.

When an institution prioritizes comfort over courage, it actively punishes the very people trying to elevate its status. We cannot build the university of tomorrow if we actively tear down the architects trying to design it.

True academic excellence requires a culture that celebrates bold risks and unconventional ideas. We must expose how this internal sabotage destroys academic hope before it destroys the institution itself.

The Procrustean Policy

In the ancient Greek myth, Procrustes made weary travelers fit his iron bed by stretching the short ones and chopping the legs off the tall ones.

That violent mythological practice has become the operational standard in too many higher education institutions today. The standard academic bed demands strict conformity from every single scholar who enters the system.

Faculty members are expected to follow the exact same path to promotion and produce the exact same forms of low-risk research. They are pressured to adopt the same predictable retirement timelines as everyone who came before them.

When a brilliant colleague attempts to build something truly new, they are met with existential resistance rather than institutional encouragement.

They might propose a global forum, an interdisciplinary laboratory, or a venture backed startup. Instead of being celebrated, they are treated as if they have committed a massive crime of differentiation. They are viewed as a threat to the comfortable equilibrium of the academic department.

"We are killing the very hope we are supposed to ignite"

I recently watched a family member attempt to create a globally unique academic forum in her specific field. She pitched the ambitious idea to the highest levels of her mid-tier university, detailing the prestige, the funding potential, and the national value. The response she received was not enthusiastic support, but rather a quiet and suffocating counsel from a senior leader.

She was asked why she dared to aspire and was told to simply enjoy being exactly like everyone else. The senior leader actually asked her if she thought she was better than her peers.

The brilliant idea was immediately shut down to preserve the fragile egos of the collective group. This is not just policy inertia, but an active campaign of internal sabotage.

The Catastrophic Cost

The Crab Bucket Climate is incredibly expensive for the global academic ecosystem. Universities operating under this climate actively drive brain drain by pushing their most creative minds out the door. The most ambitious scholars simply do not stay to be chopped down to size by their insecure peers.

They inevitably leave for agile startups or alternative institutions that reward differentiation rather than actively punish it. This toxic culture also completely suppresses the creation of high impact research.

Risk and originality are the absolute prerequisites for world class discovery and scientific advancement.

When the reward structure prioritizes conformity and safe publications, the university guarantees its permanent place in the middle tier of global education.

Academic leaders must realize that you cannot achieve extraordinary results by mandating ordinary behavior.

Most tragically, this environment deeply devalues the financial and emotional investment of our current students.

"The job of leadership is not to enforce conformity, but to maximize human potential"

Students pay for an education that is supposed to equip them for global leadership and bold innovation. Instead, they are taught by academics who have been forced to internalize extreme caution and institutional fear. We cannot expect students to change the world if their professors are terrified of changing the syllabus.

Until leadership rips this Procrustean bed out of the faculty lounge, these universities will remain self-limiting archives of the obvious.

We must aggressively dismantle these structures of suppression. We must urgently begin to reward the climbers rather than the crabs.

The Celebrity Trap

Another problem is important to explore too. This internal culture of avoiding real peer driven innovation translates directly into how we gather and share knowledge globally.

Many academic summits today start with the noble goal of bringing brilliant people together to debate and imagine something better. The intention is good.

But somewhere along the way, the summit becomes a theatrical stage, and the university simply becomes a passive audience.

The focus shifts entirely from meaningful dialogue to the star power of celebrity keynote speakers. Their personal fame becomes the primary selling point, and their mere presence becomes the main headline of the event.

Meanwhile, the highly qualified delegates who traveled and prepared to contribute are reduced to mere spectators watching someone else perform.

"A summit built only around celebrities is an event you attend, not a conversation you join"

We absolutely need great speakers to energize a room and inspire new ways of thinking. But a gathering built exclusively around celebrities stops being a true academic summit. People quickly stop coming back because no one wants to return to a place where their voice fundamentally does not matter.

The real value of any global gathering lives in the quiet and unscripted spaces in between the scheduled talks. The true value is found in the questions that challenge core assumptions and the debates that push ideas significantly further. It lives in the unexpected connections made over coffee that eventually turn into real world collaborations.

As we design the next generation of academic gatherings, we must fundamentally shift our approach to collective wisdom.

We must let the keynote speakers open the summit, but we must let the participants actually shape it. Let the delegates own the outcomes, because this is how simple summits finally transform into global movements.

[10]

BALANCE OF GENERATIONS

A world that prioritizes youth and sidelines wisdom risks repeating its mistakes loudly and with the best intentions

Creating lasting global academic movements requires the input of every generation, not just the youngest in the room. Much of the global conversation today revolves entirely around the next generation.

In policy circles, global institutions, and universities, we are constantly searching for fresh graduates and new talent.

We celebrate the boundless energy of youth, and we absolutely should. But somewhere along this rapid pursuit of the new, we forgot something fundamentally essential about human progress. We forgot that deep wisdom is an irreplaceable resource. We forgot that lived experience is a vital form of capital.

Years of dedicated service produce a profound depth that no accelerated crash course can ever teach. In our urgent rush to recruit young professionals, we actively sideline the very people who have lived through global crises. We ignore those who have built our institutions and mentored previous generations.

These seasoned professionals understand systemic complexity in a way no fresh graduate possibly can. They offer a strategic clarity that has been shaped over decades of both failure and success. They possess a real world understanding that simply cannot be searched for or generated by a machine.

The Missing Half

This stark demographic imbalance is actively harming academia and the broader global ecosystem. We see prominent international organizations launching programs exclusively for young professionals while completely ignoring their older counterparts.

They strictly recruit individuals under a certain age while dismissing those who bring decades of hard-earned institutional memory.

Major global institutions, such as the United Nations "Young Professional Program", explicitly limit applications to individuals under the age of 32, highlighting a systemic bias toward youth over seasoned experience.

That is why we must advocate for a new global initiative, I call the "Wisdom Professionals Program". This initiative would restore balance by valuing seasoned experts as vital contributors to our future rather than viewing them as past chapters of their careers. This concept is not the opposite of youth development programs.

It is the missing half of a highly functioning and healthy global system. Young professionals bring essential acceleration, but wisdom professionals bring necessary direction. Age is not a barrier to innovation, but rather a profound asset for sustainable change.

"Young professionals bring essential acceleration, and wisdom professionals bring necessary direction"

The proposed Wisdom Professionals Program advocates for structurally integrating older experts into global organizations to retain critical institutional memory and emotional maturity.

If universities and global institutions are serious about principled transformation, they must value both demographics equally. It is time to restore the full circle of human capability by pairing energy with experience and youth with depth. This careful balance of generations is exactly what the future deserves.

It is also the exact kind of balance we need when addressing the most complex scientific and technological questions of our era. When we lack the direction that comes from deep wisdom, we begin to analyze the future with a terrifying lack of soul.

The Empirical Imperative

We see this lack of soul clearly in how modern society discusses both cosmology and artificial intelligence. At its core, the scientific method is a commitment to radical honesty and the disciplined pursuit of objective reality.

It requires us to follow the data wherever it leads, regardless of our personal philosophical discomfort.

Yet in modern science, we face a strange and revealing paradox. As our observational tools advance, they reveal a universe defined by breathtaking mathematical precision.

The data overwhelmingly points away from random chaos and toward deliberate calibration.

From the fine tuning of cosmological constants to the sophisticated information structures within biological systems, we see highly specified complexity.

In any other field of inquiry, this complexity would immediately suggest intelligence as the primary cause.

However, a significant portion of the western scientific community seems determined to avoid this specific conclusion at all costs.

"If science is the unbiased interpretation of reality, then denying the appearance of design is a philosophical prejudice"

We witness enormous intellectual energy expended on constructing increasingly convoluted and untestable hypotheses. Concepts like unobservable multiverses serve primarily as escape routes from the obvious implications of the data right in front of us.

This is a massive departure from the basic scientific principle where the simplest explanation fitting the facts is usually preferred.

True scientific integrity means accepting that if the empirical evidence strongly indicates intelligence, acknowledging a "Creator" is not an abandonment of reason.

It is the most logical and intellectually honest outcome of the data. We must stop confusing the pursuit of truth with the blind pursuit of materialist alternatives to God.

A Horizon of Meaning

This same materialist blindness heavily infects our current writings on new technologies like artificial intelligence.

Much of the discourse suffers from a striking silence about faith and a tendency to erase our spiritual foundations. Some intellectuals completely erase their own cultural roots while heavily copying from Western sources.

For example, analyzing artificial intelligence only in material terms produces visions that may be technically accurate but remain spiritually empty.

The entire framework ignores the presence of the creator, who is the source of both creation and order. Without that recognition, the question of humanity's future is cut entirely in half.

We see talented people losing their orientation in a massive flood of materialism. They describe creation without acknowledging the Creator, which fundamentally misunderstands both. As holy texts clearly remind us, both the creation and the command belong entirely to the divine.

There is a deeply missing field of inquiry regarding the relationship between faith and future sciences. It is not enough to ask what algorithms can do or how they will disrupt our global labor markets. We must also ask what these technologies mean for our spiritual place in the universe.

"When the presence of the Creator is removed from how we think about the future, our imagination shrinks rather than expands"

The real challenge ahead is not only to master artificial intelligence, but to place it within a broader horizon of meaning. This horizon must explicitly include

wisdom, human conscience, and faith. To approach technology without these pillars is to risk misunderstanding not just our tools, but ourselves.

We need intellectuals and academicians to explore how spiritual frameworks can guide technological futures. This integration is not a luxury, but an absolute necessity for human survival and flourishing. The future will not be shaped by machines alone, but by whether we dare to include ethics and faith in our vision of progress.

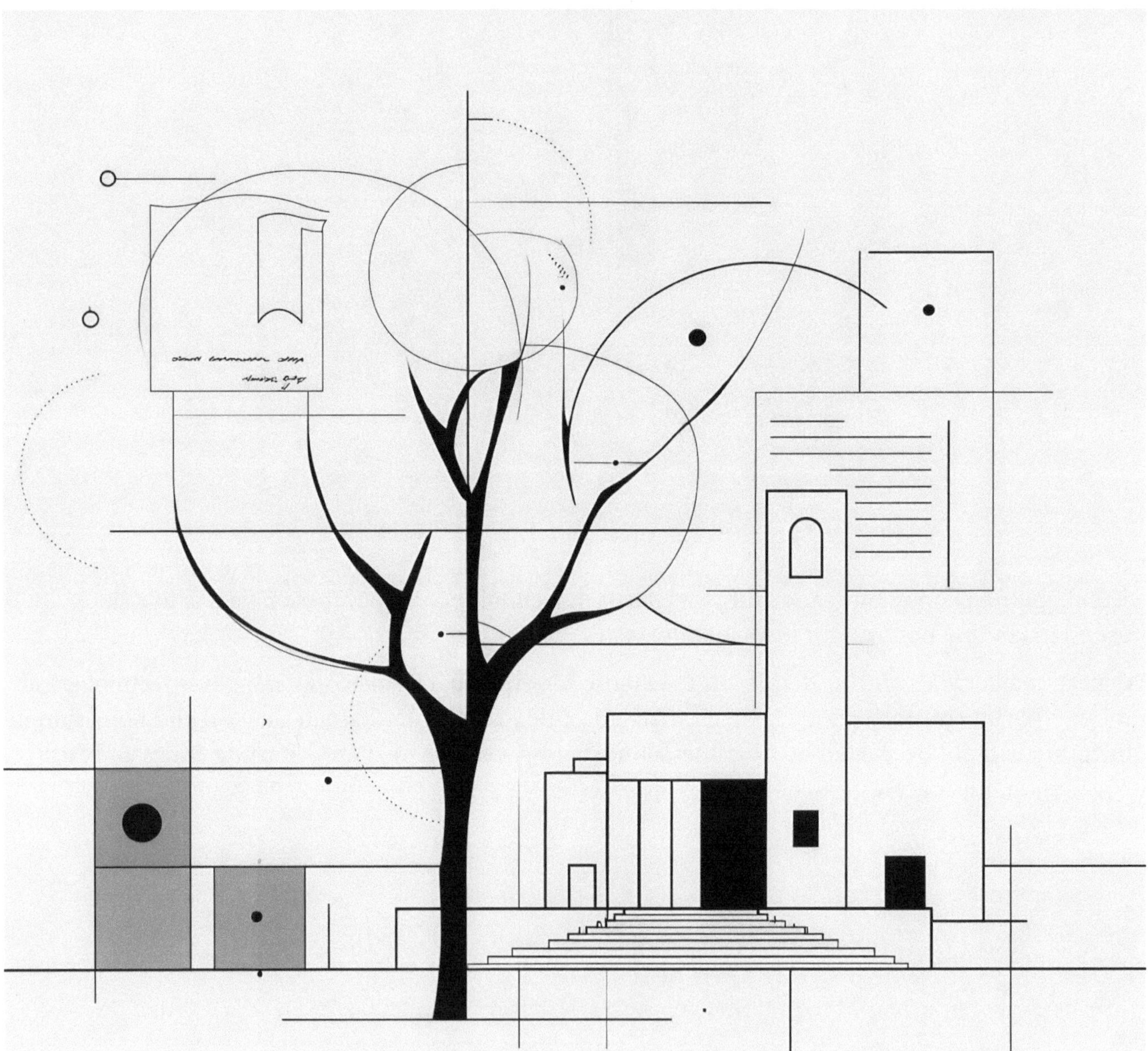

[11]

MEASURING LIFELONG LEARNING

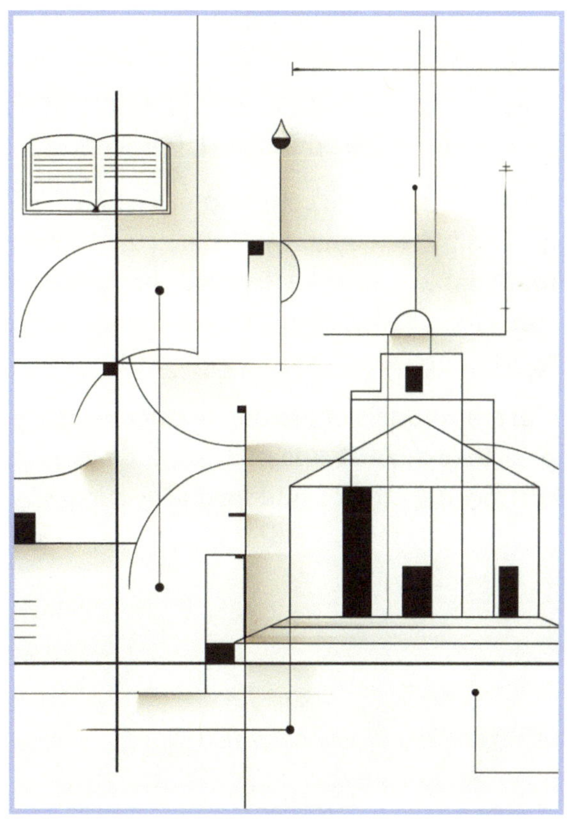

Lifelong learning is not a curriculum. It is a life lived and a wisdom earned

This soulful vision of progress must extend to how we measure the span of a person's entire existence. When we speak about lifelong learning today, we obsess almost entirely over the word "learning".

We completely forget the profound importance of the word "life". We have taken a beautiful, holistic concept of human evolution and turned it into a mechanical industrial process.

We try to measure continuous human growth by reducing it to a sterile checklist of marketable skills. We demand that professionals constantly accumulate credits, digital badges, short courses, and workshop certificates.

Current models of lifelong learning heavily prioritize quantifiable metrics, such as certificates, credits, and formal seminars, while systematically ignoring informal life experiences.

We act as if the entirety of human development can be neatly captured and evaluated in a corporate spreadsheet.

"When we try to measure learning, we reduce it to skills and certificates as if human growth can be captured in a spreadsheet"

But life teaches us far more than any formal curriculum or corporate workshop ever will. We learn profound lessons of resilience, patience, and empathy from our parents and our daily neighbors.

We absorb strategic thinking and emotional intelligence from our friends, our past jobs, and the people we love.

We gain our deepest and most enduring insights from our painful failures, our personal losses, and our quiet volunteer work. All of these messy, unscripted human experiences shape us profoundly and permanently. Yet our modern educational and corporate systems stubbornly refuse to count them.

The Spreadsheet Illusion

Our current academic and corporate systems are designed to measure only what is easily quantifiable. They meticulously track hard technical skills and occasionally attempt to measure soft skills through standardized behavioral tests. But they rarely acknowledge anything beyond the strict, artificial boundaries of the formal professional environment.

"We remove life from "lifelong learning", and then wonder why our assessments miss the full picture"

We have created a global economy that is obsessed with formal credentials rather than actual human competence. A professional might spend ten years successfully raising a family, managing complex community disputes, and navigating profound personal tragedies.

Yet our systems treat that decade as an empty gap in their resume because no corporate entity issued a formal certificate for it.

This rigid and narrow framework is exactly why we so often fail to recognize real, transformative talent. We are measuring only a tiny and highly sanitized fraction of what a human being actually learns across a lifetime. We remove the messy reality of life from lifelong learning, and then we wonder why our assessments miss the full picture.

We build hiring practices and university admissions around these severely limited metrics. We routinely discard brilliant individuals simply because their profound life experiences do not fit neatly into a digital drop down menu.

Talent is not an isolated checklist of skills that can be downloaded into a brain during a weekend seminar.

Real talent is the culmination of lived experiences colliding with personal reflection and outward action. It is the ability to navigate ambiguity, which is almost always learned through hardship rather than through textbooks.

When we ignore these uncertified lessons, we deeply impoverish our institutions and our global workforce.

The Forest and the Tree

We can understand this systemic failure by looking closely at how we evaluate the natural world. A healthy, towering tree cannot be properly assessed only by examining its seeds in an isolated laboratory.

You must look at the rich, complex soil that anchored it and the harsh sun that tested its endurance.

You must examine the surrounding trees that protected it and the broader ecosystem that nurtured or challenged its growth.

You simply cannot understand the quality and resilience of the tree if you completely ignore the forest. The exact same principle applies to human development, intellectual maturity, and true capability.

"You cannot understand the quality of the tree if you ignore the forest"

You cannot understand the depth of a human being's lifelong learning when you focus only on their formal education. A resume tells us what a person has been paid to do, but it rarely tells us what they have actually overcome.

The challenges they navigated in their personal and community lives are the true indicators of their character and judgment.

The human mind is designed to learn continuously through constant interaction with

its chaotic environment. The most profound lessons regarding ethics, patience, and strategic negotiation usually happen far away from any classroom. When we invalidate these natural learning environments, we actively discourage people from valuing their own lived experiences.

Yet we continue to blind ourselves to this rich ecosystem of human capability. We treat students and professionals as isolated units of economic production rather than complex human stories. It is time we change how we define, measure, and validate human growth.

Recognizing True Talent

If we truly want to recognize exceptional talent, we must radically overhaul our institutional lenses. In hiring, in higher education, and in global leadership, we must start seeing people as full, multidimensional stories. We must value the profound wisdom shaped by experiences that no university certificate could ever capture.

Universities today often treat lifelong learning merely as a secondary revenue stream. They aggressively market new certificates and executive master's degrees to their alumni networks.

They sell the fear of professional obsolescence rather than celebrating the natural accumulation of human wisdom.

> *"Talent is not a checklist of skills. It is a story shaped by experiences that no certificate can capture"*

This requires a shift away from automated screening systems that only scan for specific academic keywords. It requires leaders and educators who are willing to engage in deep, unstructured conversations with their candidates. We must ask people what they have survived, what they have built, and who they have served in silence.

The university of tomorrow must find ways to honor and integrate this informal, lived wisdom. It must become a place that helps individuals articulate the value of their uncertified life experiences to the broader world. True education should not erase our personal histories, but rather teach us how to leverage them for the greater good.

We must stop treating lifelong learning as an endless treadmill of mandatory corporate workshops. We must restore its original, noble meaning as the continuous unfolding of human potential. When we finally bring life back into our understanding of learning, we will unlock the true genius of our global society.

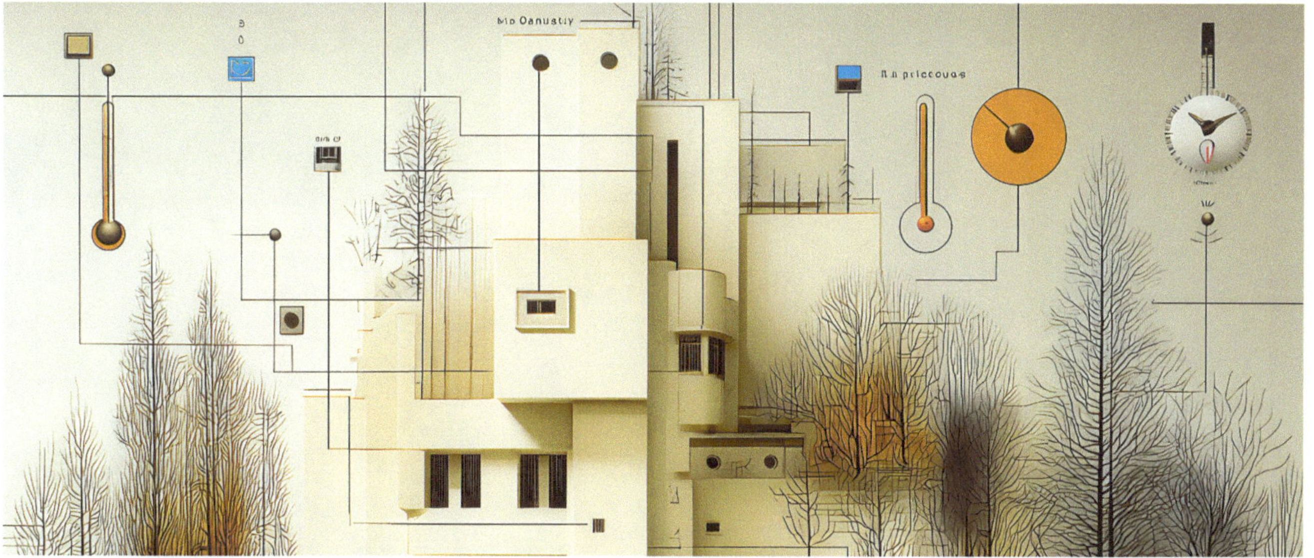

[12]

THE WAVE WILL NOT WAIT

Desire without the willpower to act simply becomes a perpetual state of complaint

Unlocking the academic collective genius requires more than just continuous conversation; it requires immediate and courageous movement. Every time we find ourselves trying to only convince one

another that change is necessary, a difficult truth emerges. It becomes painfully clear that we are not yet the actual engines of that change.

We deeply desire transformation across our global institutions, but we hesitate constantly at the edge of real action.

Desire without the willpower to act simply becomes a perpetual state of complaint. Higher education has spent far too long complaining about its own structural limitations.

We keep having the exact same circular conversation year after year without making any meaningful, systemic progress. Thought leaders spend their precious energy trying to convince reluctant faculty that the institutional crisis is completely real.

Meanwhile, academic committees spend countless hours debating whether we actually need to adapt to a changing world. This endless debate creates a false sense of productivity while the world races past us.

Our institutional governance structures are perfectly designed to slow every innovative impulse down to an absolute crawl.

They are doing exactly what they were historically built to do, which is to protect the status quo at any cost. We are watching the future arrive while we wait for permission to acknowledge it.

The Illusion of Permission

We must accept that real change in human evolution has never once waited for a formal committee vote. When a transformation becomes truly existential, asking for institutional permission becomes entirely irrelevant. The universe itself moves forward with or without our bureaucratic approval.

This is exactly where the global higher education system now stands at this critical juncture in history. The next great shift in our universities will absolutely not begin in comfortable senate chambers. It will not be initiated by cautious rectors, university presidents, or traditional academic councils.

It will rise like an undeniable tide from the bottom up, sweeping away outdated traditions. It will be led primarily by students who are simply no longer willing to accept expensive irrelevance. It will be driven by societies that demand tangible value and practical solutions to their daily struggles.

It will be championed by bold visionaries who sense what is coming long before institutions are ready to speak it aloud. This massive wave of change is not a theoretical concept debated endlessly in academic journals. It is not a distant possibility waiting patiently for us in some faraway decade.

It is already forming right now, gathering immense power just beneath the surface of our current reality. The signals are everywhere for those who choose to open their eyes and observe the shifting landscape. We must stop pretending that our prestigious history will magically protect us from future irrelevance.

Learning from Antalya!

I currently live in Antalya, Turkiye, and I observed an important lesson from this city that we can learn about intentional transformation. Every autumn, when the last tourists depart (20 million of them come every year), and the Mediterranean softens into silence, something remarkable begins. The streets grow quieter, but the foundational spirit of the city grows significantly stronger.

Antalya does not rest or stagnate during this quiet and unobserved off season. It actively rebuilds, renews, and meticulously plans for the future demands of the coming year. The soul of the city springs into action, restoring its infrastructure and preparing to welcome the entire world once again.

This beautiful cycle of intentional renewal is exactly the spirit behind the idea of constant gradual change and fine-tuning that we need in higher education. If we observe that much of the academic world slows its pace and clings to tradition, we must do the exact opposite. We must spring into bold action by building deep, meaningful partnerships across two hundred different countries.

We must prepare a massive global infrastructure that represents over thirty five thousand universities and hundreds of millions of students. Antalya can teach us that great accomplishments and lasting change are never truly spontaneous occurrences. They are the deliberate result of hard work done when absolutely no one is watching.

It is the heavy stones laid in winter and the seeds planted in silence that create a beautiful spring. It is the visionary focus held firmly during the quiet season that guarantees monumental future success. We must share this profound commitment to intentional renewal, academic excellence, and deep societal purpose.

The Final Choice

Universities can be the corner stone of building something incredibly significant for the future of human wisdom and global collaboration. We must finally stop managing the current gentle decline of an old system and start designing the architecture of a new one.

The future of the university depends entirely on leaders who are willing to take bold risks today.

As this massive wave of educational transformation approaches, humanity faces a very stark division. Some bold institutions will choose to step forward and actively lead this necessary revolution. Many traditional institutions will fight desperately to resist it and protect their familiar, fading comforts.

But absolutely no one will be able to stop this wave from washing over the entire global educational landscape. The ultimate question is no longer whether you personally believe this disruption is happening. The evidence is already overwhelming and undeniably visible everywhere we look in modern society.

"The question is not whether you believe it. The question is whether you will be ready to lead it"

The real question is whether you will be ready to courageously lead this movement when it arrives at your campus. Or at the very least, whether you will be ready to join it when you finally see it coming. We must prepare ourselves, our students, and our institutions for a radically different tomorrow.

We must leave the safety of our academic fortresses and fully rejoin the dynamic, messy reality of the world. The future of human progress is calling us to be courageous, imaginative, and deeply purposeful once again. This massive wave of change will absolutely not wait for a committee approval.

EPILOGUE

THE STORY CONTINUES

This book was written in anticipation, but the next chapters must be written in action

We have reached the final pages of these notes, but we have certainly not reached the end of our shared journey. Everything we have discussed in this book exists in the quiet pause before a necessary global transformation.

We have outlined the deep challenges facing our academic institutions and the beautiful opportunities that lie just ahead.

We named this collection of thoughts "The University of Tomorrow" for a very specific reason.

The future of global higher education .. the university of tomorrow .. will not be solved by a single author or a single prestigious institution. It will be solved by the collective courage of educators and leaders who choose to step forward.

A Shared Responsibility

For too long, the narrative of academic excellence has been dictated by a narrow fraction of the world. We have allowed a small group of self-proclaimed "elite" institutions to define what success looks like for everyone else. But the vast majority of human potential is nurtured in the thousands of universities that rarely make the international news or the ranking reports.

These unranked institutions are important and essential components of the true engines of global progress. They are the places where local problems are solved and where communities are actually lifted out of darkness.

The responsibility to re-imagine the university belongs to all of us, not just to those sitting comfortably at the top of a ranking table.

"The future of the university belongs to those who show up where humanity is actually growing"

We must stop waiting for permission from outdated governance structures or external accreditation bodies. We must actively reclaim the soul of our institutions by prioritizing wisdom over mere information and human connection over mechanical metrics. The wave of change is already here, and it demands that we finally rejoin the reality of the world.

The Need to Meet!

This profound need for collective action is exactly why we are building the "World Summit on Universities, WSU". In the near future, the beautiful coastal city of Antalya will proudly, and annually, welcome the global academic community and its stakeholders. It will be a historic gathering designed not to celebrate our past, but to intentionally design our future.

Like the city of Antalya itself, which constantly rebuilds and renews its spirit, we must enter our own season of bold preparation. We must build a massive global infrastructure that represents every corner of the academic ecosystem. We aspire to bring the forgotten majority of universities to the center of the global conversation.

"Great modernization and lasting change are never spontaneous. They are built intentionally."

We hope that when the world of academia gathers in such a global summit, we will not simply attend another passive event filled with celebrity keynote speakers. We will arrive as active participants ready to shape the outcomes and take ownership of our shared destiny. We will sit together to answer the uncomfortable questions we have avoided for far too long.

The Open Door

You do not need to be a university president to be part of this necessary revolution. Whether you are a student, a seasoned wisdom professional, or an educator frustrated by the crab bucket climate, your voice is essential. We invite you to walk through this open door and join us in this critical work.

We will continue to write, to listen, and to share our reflections as this global movement grows. But the most important words will not be found in the pages of any published book. They will be found in the courageous actions you take within your own classrooms and communities tomorrow.

The opportunity to revive the soul of the university is entirely ours. Let us turn toward the future with clear eyes, open hearts, and an unwavering commitment to human wisdom. Thank you for reading, and we look forward to welcoming you to the next chapter.

Prof. Bassem Khafagy
Antalya, Turkiye, Mach 2026

ABOUT THE BOOK

University of Tomorrow

Reclaiming the Soul & Meaning of Academia

University of Tomorrow challenges the global higher education system to urgently rediscover its existential purpose. In an era where artificial intelligence has made raw knowledge abundant, the book argues that universities must radically evolve. They must transition from being mere providers of information into deliberate designers of human wisdom and curators of meaning.

The book offers a profound call to action by dismantling rigid bureaucratic structures and rejecting toxic internal cultures of mediocrity. It urges educators and leaders to leave their academic fortresses and actively engage with the massive demographic shifts shaping our future. This work is an invitation to reclaim the soul of academia before our institutions become highly efficient but fundamentally irrelevant.

ABOUT THE SERIES

Notes on Re-Imagining University (Vol. 01)

This book is Volume 01 in the Notes on Re-Imagining University series. It began as a collection of public reflections aimed at challenging the comfortable status quo of global higher education. The series exists to ask the uncomfortable questions that academic institutions often avoid.

Future volumes will continue to explore the profound intersection of technology, human wisdom, and global demographic shifts. The ultimate goal of this series is to build a unified voice for the vast and forgotten majority of the global academic ecosystem. We must actively champion all the thirty-five thousand institutions that truly, and collectively, hold the academic world together, rather than focusing solely on a narrow self-proclaimed "elite" tier.

ABOUT THE AUTHOR

Prof. Bassem Khafagy

Prof. Bassem Khafagy serves as the Secretary General of the World Universities Foundation. He has spent over four decades working within and supporting global higher education across different systems and countries. His lifelong mission is to redefine the future of learning by integrating human wisdom with advanced technological innovation.

As a prominent keynote speaker and bestselling author, he actively challenges academic leadership to break free from traditional constraints. His work focuses on strategies to re-imagine the university, ethical artificial intelligence integration, and the urgent need to build a collaborative global ecosystem.

He writes with deep conviction about the responsibility that arises when an institution stops asking how to survive and starts asking how to matter.

www.ingramcontent.com/pod-product-compliance
Lightning Source LLC
LaVergne TN
LVHW070216110826
845147LV00003B/588
9781889626260

"The university of tomorrow cannot survive as a content provider. It must become a context provider."

Notes on Re-Imagining University vol. 01

Global higher education is facing a profound crisis of imagination. With over 264 million students across 35,000 institutions, the academic world has become obsessed with sterile rankings. Meanwhile, the rapid advancement of artificial intelligence has made raw information and basic intelligence as abundant as water.

In this disrupted era, the traditional university cannot survive merely as a content provider. It must radically rediscover its fundamental value to society. *University of Tomorrow: Reclaiming the Soul & Meaning of Academia* is a powerful call to fundamentally rethink the purpose of higher education.

Prof. Bassem Khafagy argues that institutions must evolve from being gatekeepers of scarce facts into deliberate designers of human wisdom. He challenges the rigid bureaucratic structures and toxic internal cultures that currently suffocate true academic innovation. The book demands that we finally empower the forgotten majority of unranked universities that actually solve local problems.

We must stop managing the gentle decline of an old educational system. It is time to start actively designing the architecture of a new one. The future of human progress is calling us to be courageous once again.

To Order:
www.wuf.global

DERRICK NAPIER

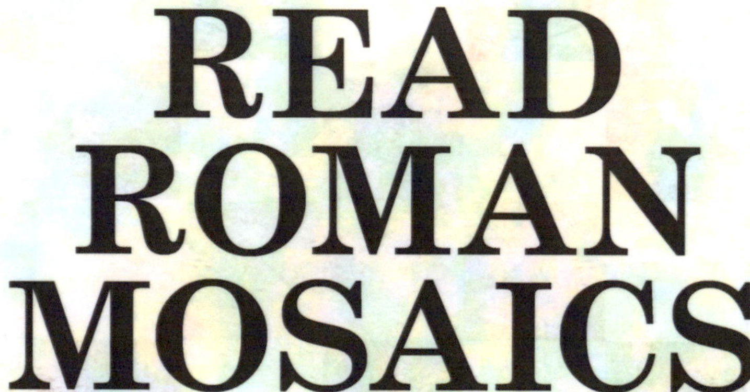

READ ROMAN MOSAICS

BIGNOR, LULLINGSTONE, CHEDWORTH, BRADING & NEWPORT ROMAN VILLAS